8/3/84
To Tina
Chill out
with my penguins

PENGUINS AT HOME
GENTOOS OF ANTARCTICA

written and photo-illustrated by
Bruce McMillan

Port Lockroy, Wiencke Island,
Palmer Archipelago

Houghton Mifflin Company   Boston   1993

This book was photographed on the Antarctic Peninsula and its surrounding islands during January and February 1992. Travel aboard the MV Illiria and its zodiacs, under the direction of Darrel Schoeling, was coordinated and provided in part by ⊜ Travel Dynamics, 132 East 70th Street, New York, New York 10021.

Penguin facts were verified by Antarctic penguin field researchers David Freeland Parmelee and Susan G. Trivelpiece.

Photographic Data
Cameras: Nikon F4/MF23 and FE2 with 24 mm, 50 mm, 180 mm, and 300 mm AF Nikkor lenses and sometimes a circular polarizing filter
Tripod: Bogen Professional 3001 with 3025 head
Film: Kodachrome 64 processed by Kodalux

Designed by Bruce McMillan
Text set in Sabon   Title Text set in Sabon Bold
Color separations by General Graphic Services
Printed on Command Satin
Printed and bound by Horowitz/Rae
Printed in the United States of America
HOR 10 9 8 7 6 5 4 3 2 1

Library of Congress Cataloging-in-Publication Data

McMillan, Bruce.
   Penguins at home : gentoos of Antarctica / written and photo-illustrated by Bruce McMillan.
        p.   cm.
   Includes bibliographical references (p. 32) and index.
   Summary: Describes the physical characteristics, behavior, and life cycle of the timid gentoo penguin.
   ISBN 0-395-66560-4
   1. Gentoo penguin—Antarctic regions—Juvenile literature.
[1. Gentoo penguin.   2. Penguins.]   I. Title.
QL696.S473M39   1993
598´.441—dc20   92-34769 CIP AC

Gentoo *(JEN-too)*

Many people visit penguins at zoos, but few are able to see them at home in the wild. Home for three kinds of penguins is surrounded by the stormiest ocean on earth; Adélies (*Pygoscelis adeliae*), Chinstraps (*Pygoscelis antarctica*), and Southern Gentoos (*Pygoscelis papua elsworthii*) live on the icy-cold Antarctic Peninsula and its nearby islands. The largest of these penguins, 2½ feet tall (76 centimeters) when fully grown, are the Southern Gentoos. They're also the gentlest and most timid of the three species.

brush-tail

Gentoos are Brush-tail penguins. All Brush-tails—Adélies, Chinstraps, and Gentoos—have tails with longer feathers than those of other kinds of penguins. Gentoos sometimes shake their brush-tails around in the air when swimming at the surface, but when they swim underwater they use their pointed tails and feet to steer. They don't use their feet to paddle like ducks do. Gentoos use something else to speed themselves along.

flippers

Waterboat Point, Paradise Harbor, Antarctic Peninsula

Gentoos—and all other penguins—have wings called flippers to propel themselves forward. They "fly" underwater. Unlike the wings of most birds, penguins' wings don't fold, and the bones in them are solid, not hollow. Their wings are built for swimming, and Gentoos spend much of their time swimming—especially in the winter.

The dark, frigid Antarctic winter lasts from June through August. But in November, which is springtime here at the bottom of the world, the daylight hours get longer—much longer. Southern Gentoos live only hundreds of miles from the South Pole, where the summer sun never sets. When Gentoos come splashing ashore in November, it's for a reason.

walking

It's the start of the Gentoo breeding season. Like all true sea birds, Gentoos come ashore to breed and molt. Walking like human babies who are just learning to stand and step, they waddle over rocks and ice and snow. Unlike most birds, penguins stand straight up. They use their "arms"—flippers—for balance. As they climb up penguin-worn trails, they look like circus tightrope walkers.

There are no land predators here in Antarctica, so adult Gentoos have nothing to fear. They climb to exposed, flat nesting areas. Some areas are only a few feet from the water's edge, but others are on ridges as much as 150 feet (45 meters) above sea level.

rookery

Cuverville Island, Errera Channel, Antarctic Peninsula

The nesting area where penguins gather to breed is called a colony or rookery. Of the three Brush-tails, Gentoos live in the smallest rookery groups. One of the largest Gentoo rookeries has 2,000 breeding pairs, while Adélie rookeries have as many as 100,000 breeding pairs. Gentoos space their nests farther apart— about 3½ feet (1 meter) from each other. A rookery may seem crowded with penguins, but in ice-covered Antarctica there are few open places for nesting. Sometimes Gentoos must even share their rookery with Adélies and Chinstraps.

nests

These rookeries are where Gentoos make their homes for the summer. Many of them stay with the same mate at the same rookery year after year, though sometimes they select another rookery to raise their family. At their home site both male and female make a nest out of one of the few building materials available in Antarctica—small rocks. Each nest's bowl-like shape not only fits the penguin's round belly; it also keeps the eggs from rolling away. Every day, Gentoos go to sea to feed, but at night they return to their nests.

Almirante Brown Station, Paradise Harbor, Antarctic Peninsula

One day the female Gentoo doesn't leave her nest. She settles there to stay, and five days later she lays her first egg. Three days after that, she lays a second egg. Now, the hungry mother-to-be, who hasn't eaten in more than a week, can leave to feed at sea while the father-to-be takes over the nesting duties.

Both adult penguins share these nesting duties. They incubate the eggs, covering them with their bodies to keep each growing life warm. A "scorchingly hot" summer day here is only 45°F (7°C). Nesting also protects the eggs from attack by Skuas (*SKEW-ahs*), birds that look like large, brown sea gulls. Skuas (*Catharacta maccormicki* and *Catharacta lonnbergi*) eat penguin eggs and even unattended chicks.

stones

Each nest is the exclusive family territory for that pair of Gentoo parents-to-be. At this time of year, Gentoos wander around the rookery in search of more stones to add to their nests. They are notorious stone thieves, always ready to snatch one from another nest. They carry the stones, one by one, in their bills. When they arrive back at their nests, they drop the stones onto them, sometimes not even disturbing the nesting penguin. These small rocks are continually stolen and moved from one nest to another, then stolen yet again.

climbing down

Cuverville Island, Errera Channel, Antarctic Peninsula

Some of the younger, inexperienced Gentoo parents-to-be may have selected nesting sites that now have problems. But the older Gentoos have likely chosen areas that aren't flooding from melting ice, nor getting covered by drifting snow.

Nesting and feeding are full-time jobs. When it's time to go to sea for food, one of the Gentoo pair stays on the nest while the other begins climbing down over slippery rocks. Gentoos usually make their comical walk to the sea under cloudy skies. Though the center of the Antarctic continent is the driest place in the world, it's very different on the Antarctic Peninsula. Often it snows here, or, if it's a "warm" summer day, it rains.

porpoising

Once in the water, penguins are sleek swimmers. Their bodies are perfectly shaped for underwater speed. Their wings—flippers—aren't very big because they don't have to lift the weight of their bodies, like airborne bird wings. Buoyant water lifts the penguins, while their flippers speed them along. Gentoos are the fastest penguin swimmers, and they zip along underwater at speeds estimated as fast as 27 miles per hour (45 kilometers per hour).

They need to come up for air, so they breathe while porpoising. Gentoos, like all penguins, pop out of the water like slippery watermelon seeds. As they coast through the air, they take quick breaths to restore their oxygen, and just before slipping back into the ocean they exhale.

resting at sea

Cuverville Island, Errera Channel, Antarctic Peninsula

Gentoos may stop and spend a little time resting at sea on a piece of ice. They are comfortable standing here even though their feet are bare.

Once back in the water, Gentoos dive deep for food. They are superior divers. When underwater, their hearts beat slower and this allows them to stay under for as long as two minutes—longer than either Adélies or Chinstraps. Because Gentoos can dive more than 492 feet (150 meters) deep, which is deeper than the other two Brush-tails, they find food closer to home at greater depths. So they don't travel more than 16 miles (25.8 kilometers) from home.

krill hunting

Gentoo parents feed mostly on krill, small pink shellfish that look like miniature shrimp. They also eat a few fish and squid. But Gentoos are not the only krill seekers. Krill is the major food source in the Antarctic Ocean; Baleen whales, seals, and other penguins also eat krill. Leopard seals, though they mostly feed on krill, eat swimming penguins, too.

When Gentoos are krill hunting, they see very well underwater. Parts of their eyes, their retinas, are extremely sensitive to violet, blue, and green, the colors they find underwater. Once above the water's surface, they can't see as well.

feathers

Port Lockroy, Wiencke Island, Palmer Archipelago

    Gentoos are hot when they return from feeding, even though they've been swimming in the frigid Antarctic Ocean. They're like youngsters who come in from playing in their waterproof snowsuits—but they can't take them off. Keeping warm in Antarctica isn't the Gentoos' problem: they have trouble keeping *cool*. The unique feathers that cover their bodies—70 feathers per square inch (455 per square centimeter)—are so fine that penguins look like they're covered with fur. These feathers trap an insulating layer of air for warmth. Under their skin a layer of fat—blubber—adds even more insulation. One way penguins can cool down is to hold their flippers out in the chilly air.

preening

The undersides of Gentoo flippers are always pink after an active swim at sea. This color is from a concentration of blood vessels that expand and allow more blood to flow. When Gentoos hold out their flippers, excess heat is carried from their bodies to the flippers and is then released to the surrounding air.

While standing around after an active swim, Gentoos often do some maintenance on their waterproof "suits." They do something all birds do: they care for their feathers by preening—smoothing and picking at them. Like all birds, their lives depend on well-maintained feathers.

feet

Port Lockroy, Wiencke Island, Palmer Archipelago

Another way Gentoos cool down is by ruffling their feathers. Through ruffling, cooler air replaces the warm air trapped next to the body by overlapping feathers. The overlapping helps to make the Gentoo "suits" waterproof. Gentoos fully waterproof themselves by covering their feathers with an oil made in a gland at the base of their brush-tails. They spread the waterproofing oil over their feathers with convenient tools—their bills.

Sometimes, to scratch those hard-to-reach places, they use other tools—their feet. Not only are they good for scratching, penguin feet provide yet another way to get rid of extra heat after swimming. The blood vessels in them expand, and that's why Gentoo feet look especially pink when they come ashore.

hopping

After cooling down, it's time to return to the nest. Gentoos don't move with the grace of ballet dancers, but they do something similar. Like all penguins, they actually tiptoe on their three "toes." And when the only way up from the water is over ocean-smoothed boulders, they must do more than just walk on their "toes." They must climb by hopping from rock to rock to rock before reaching the penguin trails that lead to their rookeries.

Port Lockroy, Wiencke Island, Palmer Archipelago

Penguins are often heard before they're seen. Gentoos point their bills in the air and trumpet, *"Ah, ahaa, ahaa, aheee!"* Their loud calls sound like donkeys braying. Often their calling is to announce that they're home. Their voices, a mixed chorus of brays, carry a great distance. Since penguins "talk," they must also "listen." Just as people can recognize each other's distinct voices, penguins can recognize each other by their "voices," too. Though male and female Gentoos may look the same, with their calls they know who's who.

newborn chicks

Waterboat Point, Paradise Harbor, Antarctic Peninsula

After thirty-five days of incubation, the eggs hatch. Both Gentoo parents care for the downy-gray, newborn chicks. They take twelve-hour nesting shifts to keep their babies warm and dry. A chick's newborn down can't keep it warm enough in the cold nest of rocks. Nor can the down feathers keep the chick dry because, unlike those of its parents, a chick's feathers aren't waterproof. The nesting parents must protect their chicks with "umbrellas"—their own warm, waterproof bodies.

feeding

Chicks are always hungry and they know where to find their food. They peck at the doors of their baby food "cabinets"—their parents' bills. Parents force the food they've eaten at sea, which is now partially digested, back up their throats. The regurgitated food for the chicks' feeding is almost all solid krill or fish. With the chick's head in the parent's mouth, it looks like the chick is being eaten by the parent, but it's actually the chick who is doing the eating. This way, other birds such as Sheathbills (*Chionis alba*) are unable to steal the food. Sheathbills often wander around the rookeries and disturb feeding sessions in order to steal a spilled meal.

dirty

It's easy to spot the Gentoos who have been around the nesting area for a while. It's also easy to see which part of their bellies they lie on. The "dirty" area on their white bellies might look like a grass stain, but it's not. It comes from either green algae or green "droppings." There is little soil here in Antarctica, and only a few plants—mostly moss or lichens. Southern Gentoos live their whole lives and never see a tree. However, microscopic plants—algae—grow on the snow. The "dirty" green might be from green algae, or from the "droppings" of penguins who have been fasting. Only when penguins don't eat for a while are their "droppings" green. Usually their "droppings" are pink from the krill that they eat.

countershading

Port Lockroy, Wiencke Island, Palmer Archipelago

Dirty and clean, coming and going, back and forth—that's the life of a Gentoo at nesting time. Gentoos are always going to the ocean for food. Like many sea birds, penguins have white breasts and dark backs—countershading—that helps them stay hidden from both predators and prey at sea. Underwater, their black backs blend in with the dark bottom. Leopard seals, who attack and eat swimming Gentoos, have a harder time finding the penguins when looking down. Penguin-white undersides blend in with the sky, so Gentoo prey, like fish or krill, may not see the Gentoo's attack coming from above. The fish or krill can't escape in time to avoid becoming a penguin meal.

headband

Gentoos have white patches above their eyes that connect in a thin white line across the top of their otherwise black heads. The adults look like they're wearing an eye-to-eye headband, but the downy chicks have yet to grow and "wear" theirs. Most birds recognize other members of their species by the feather patterns on their heads and upper bodies. No other species of penguins has this unique headband marking, so when Gentoos are swimming under water or standing on land, they can probably distinguish other Gentoos from Adélies or Chinstraps by their distinctive headbands.

climbing back up

Cuverville Island, Errera Channel, Antarctic Peninsula

Climbing back up to the rookery as they've often done before, Gentoos are full of food for their chicks. It's common for them to stop along the way. Antarctica is mostly a blue and white world, but penguins sometimes find themselves climbing over pink-colored snow. Microscopic pink algae makes some glacial cliffs look like they've been sprayed with pink paint. However, this is not the same pink found on the penguins' trails and on the rocks in their rookeries— that slippery pink is from their "droppings."

guano *(GWAH-no)*

Port Lockroy, Wiencke Island, Palmer Archipelago

Fortunately for penguins, they have a poor sense of smell. The strong aroma at a rookery can be detected by humans from a half-mile at sea. It's the ammonia stench of penguin "droppings"—guano. Gentoo rookeries and trails are covered in slippery, light pink guano. Penguins, both adults and chicks, squirt their "droppings" from their backsides. Sometimes these "squirts" land on penguin neighbors a few feet away, which is another reason why penguins in rookeries look dirty. With guano everywhere, a chick's new down doesn't stay clean for long.

Port Lockroy, Wiencke Island, Palmer Archipelago

Wearing gray-and-white down feathers, growing chicks begin to look more like black-and-white adults—"dirty" adults who haven't been swimming. When a "clean" Gentoo parent returns from sea with food, the parent calls out to its chicks. But many hungry chicks run to greet the food-bearer. They all want to get into the baby food "cabinet." So the overwhelmed adult turns away, and the chicks—including its own—chase after the adult. It's a futile chase for most of them because a Gentoo parent will only feed its own chicks. Since chicks can recognize their parent's "voice" and, therefore, know they will be fed, they don't give up the chase and after awhile they are the only ones left to eat the meal.

older chicks

Nesting may be over, but these older chicks still can't leave the rookery to swim. It will be eight weeks before they grow adult feathers and are ready to go in the ocean. Their down feathers would become waterlogged now, and they would drown. So until they grow their waterproof feathers, these older chicks can only stand around, eat, and wait. They gather in groups called creches. Grouping together helps protect them from the threatening Skuas who prefer attacking solitary chicks. Once they can swim, young Gentoos still return for a meal. Their parents will feed them regurgitated food until they learn to hunt for their own krill and fish.

end of summer

Waterboat Point, Paradise Harbor, Antarctic Peninsula

At the end of summer, which is also the end of the Gentoo breeding season, parents feed at sea and then come ashore to stay. It's time for their annual molt. For three weeks they don't eat. They stand around, shed their old feathers, and wait for a new set to grow in. Once they "put on their new snowsuits"—grow their new waterproof feathers—they can swim and fish again. These feathers will last them through the coming frigid winter and will keep them warm during winter swims in the ocean. Next spring, Gentoos will be wearing the same black-and-white feather "suits" when their breeding season starts again and they raise another family in their Antarctic homes.

Southern Gentoo
(Pygoscelis papua elsworthii)

Adélie
(Pygoscelis adéliae)

Chinstrap
(Pygoscelis antarctica)

ANTARCTIC
BRUSH-TAIL PENGUINS

All eighteen species of penguins live in the bottom half of the world. Only four species truly live in Antarctica: the three Brush-tail penguins—except for the Northern Gentoo subspecies (*Pygoscelis papua papua*)—and the Emperor penguin (*Aptenodytes forsteri*). Brush-tails breed during the Antarctic summer and live in the "warmer" areas. Emperors, the largest penguins, breed during the Antarctic winter, and live in the "colder" areas.

Brush-tails have distinctive feather head-markings. Adélies have a circle of white surrounding each eye, Gentoos have a white headband from eye to eye, and Chinstraps have a thin black "chin strap."

Some species of Antarctic penguins appear to have increased in number over the past fifty years. One theory suggests that the increase is due to less competition for food. Whale and seal hunting by humans reduced these populations, which seemed to leave more krill—food—for the penguins. Another, more recent theory suggests that the penguin population increase is a result of global warming—the greenhouse effect. Though it may be a natural cyclical occurrence, it's also possible that today's global warming is due to, or has been increased by, human actions around the world. During the past fifty years this warming has led to a loss of sea-pack ice in Antarctica, possibly affecting some penguins' wintering habits and also increasing their winter survival rates. Either way, it appears there are more penguins in Antarctica today. It's ironic that this may be a result of past—seemingly unrelated—human activities.

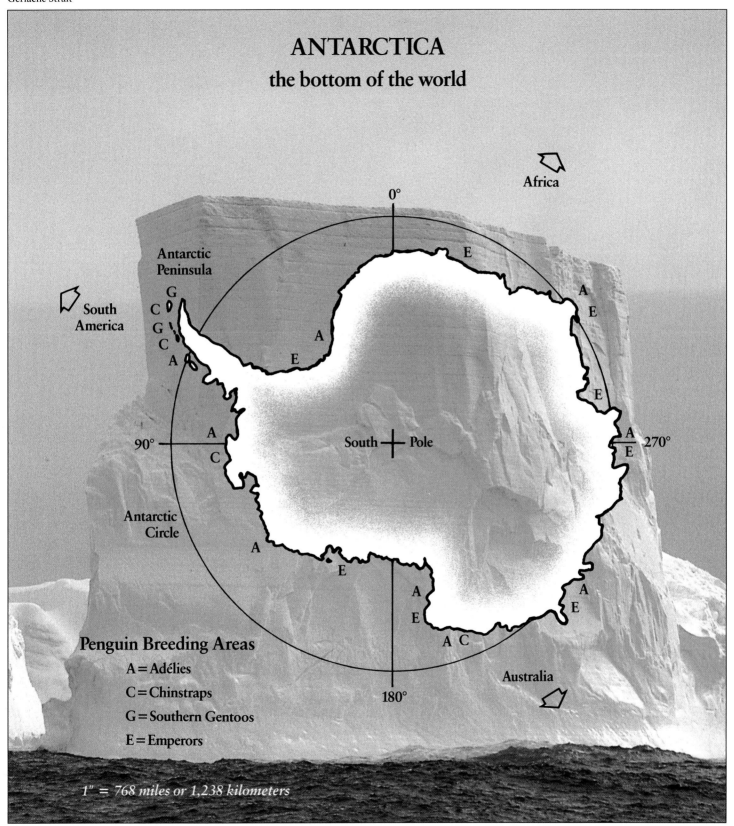

ANTARCTICA
the bottom of the world

Africa

0°

Antarctic
Peninsula

G

South
America

C

G

C

A

A

E

A

E

A

E

90°

A

C

South ┼ Pole

A
E
270°

Antarctic
Circle

E

A

A
E

A
E

A C

A
E

E

Penguin Breeding Areas

A = Adélies

C = Chinstraps

G = Southern Gentoos

E = Emperors

Australia

180°

1" = 768 miles or 1,238 kilometers

Index   Page headings **bold**

Algae, 22
  green, 22
  pink, 25
Antarctic Ocean, 14, 15
Antarctic Peninsula, 2, 3, 11, 31 (*map*)
Bill, 10, 17, 19, 21
Birds, *see also* penguins
  Sheathbill, 21
  Skua, 9, 28
Breeding season, 6, 29
Brush-tail, 4, 17
Brush-tail penguins
  Adélie, 3, 4, 7, 13, 24, 30, 31 (*map*)
  Chinstrap, 3, 4, 7, 13, 24, 30, 31 (*map*)
  Northern Gentoo, 30
  Southern Gentoo, 3, 5, 22, 31 (*map*)
Calling, 19
Chicks, *see also* feeding
  color, 20, 27
  creche, 28
  newborn, 20
  older, 28
Climbing back up, 25
Climbing down, 11
Countershading, 23
Dirty, 22, 23, 26, 27
"Droppings," *see* guano
Eggs, 8, 9, 20
  incubating, 9, 20
End of summer, *see also* seasons, **29**
Feathers, 15
  adult, 23, 27–29
  color, 20, 23, 27, 29
  down, 20, 26, 28

insulation, 15, 17
molt, 29
oil, 17
preening, 16
tail, 4
waterproof, 17, 20, 28, 29
Feeding, *see also* krill hunting, 11, 14, 15, **21,**
  28, 30
  adults, 14
  chicks, 21, 27
Feet, 4, 13, **17**
  "toes," 18
Flippers, 5, 6, 12, 15, 16
  "arms," 6
Gentoo, *see also* Penguins, **3**
Guano ("droppings"), 22, 25, **26**
  green, 22
  pink, 22, 25, 26
Headband, 4, 24, 30
Hopping, 18
Hungry chicks, *see also* feeding, **27**
Krill, 14, 21–23, 28, 30
Krill hunting, 14, 28
Leopard seals, 14, 23
Nests, 8, 9–11, 18, 20
Nesting area, *see* rookery
Newborn chicks, *see also* chicks, **20**
Oil
  gland, 17
  waterproofing, 17
Older chicks, *see also* chicks, **28**
Penguins
  Adélie, 3, 4, 7, 11, 24, 30, 31 (*map*)
  Brush-tail, 4, 7, 13, 30

Chinstrap, 3, 4, 7, 13, 24, 30, 31 (*map*)
Emperor, 30, 31 (*map*)
Northern Gentoo, 30
Southern Gentoo, 3, 5, 22, 31 (*map*)
Porpoising, *see* swimming, **12**
Predators, 9, 23
  land, 6
Preening, *see* feathers, **16**
Prey, 23
Resting at sea, 13
Rocks, *see also* stones, 6, 8, 10, 11, 20, 25
Rookery, 6, 7, 8, 10, 18, 21, 22, 25, 26, 28
  smell, 26
Seasons
  spring, 5, 29
  summer, 5, 8, 9, 11, 29, 30
  winter, 5, 29, 30
Sheathbill, *see* birds
Skua, *see* birds
South Pole, 5, 31 (*map*)
Stones, 10
Swimming, 4, 5, 12, 14–17, 23, 24, 28, 29
  breathing, 12
  diving, 13
  porpoising, 12
  speed, 12
  steering, 4
"Voice," *see also* calling, 19, 27
Walking, 6, 11, 18
  hop, 18
  toes, 18
  waddle, 6
Whales, 14, 30
Wings, *see also* flippers, 5, 12

Gerlache Strait

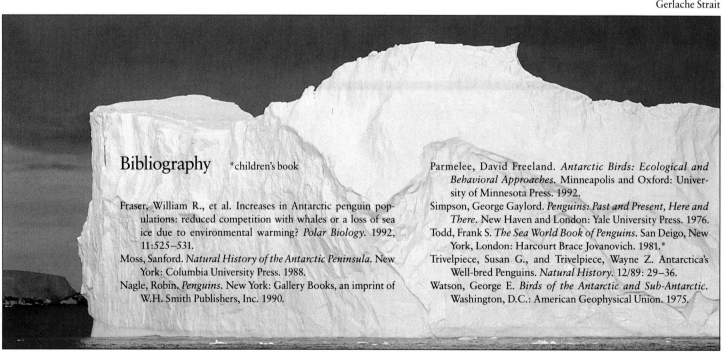

Bibliography   *children's book

Fraser, William R., et al. Increases in Antarctic penguin populations: reduced competition with whales or a loss of sea ice due to environmental warming? *Polar Biology.* 1992, 11:525–531.

Moss, Sanford. *Natural History of the Antarctic Peninsula.* New York: Columbia University Press. 1988.

Nagle, Robin. *Penguins.* New York: Gallery Books, an imprint of W.H. Smith Publishers, Inc. 1990.

Parmelee, David Freeland. *Antarctic Birds: Ecological and Behavioral Approaches.* Minneapolis and Oxford: University of Minnesota Press. 1992.

Simpson, George Gaylord. *Penguins: Past and Present, Here and There.* New Haven and London: Yale University Press. 1976.

Todd, Frank S. *The Sea World Book of Penguins.* San Deigo, New York, London: Harcourt Brace Jovanovich. 1981.*

Trivelpiece, Susan G., and Trivelpiece, Wayne Z. Antarctica's Well-bred Penguins. *Natural History.* 12/89: 29–36.

Watson, George E. *Birds of the Antarctic and Sub-Antarctic.* Washington, D.C.: American Geophysical Union. 1975.

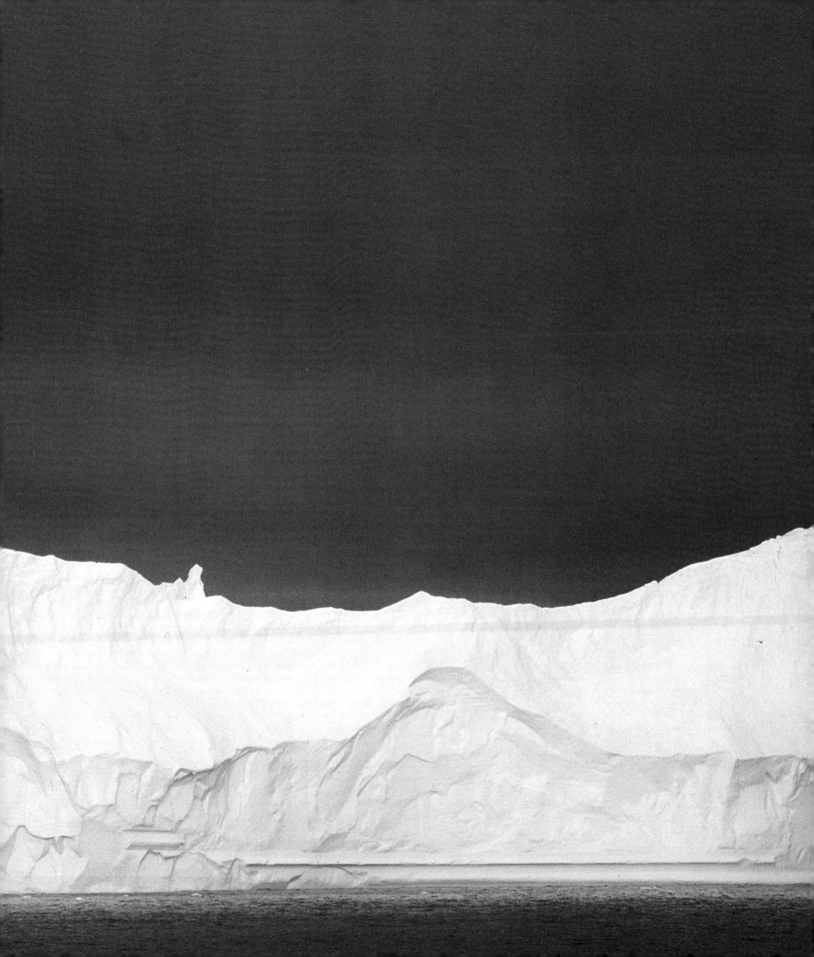